How to Reclaim Your Energy

By

Kirsten Ivatts

Dedicated to Silvia Hartmann

A true genius in an age of madness.

How to Reclaim Your Energy

Copyright Kirsten Ivatts 2021

Contents

Foreword

Last year I created a small correspondence course to teach people how to take back their energy from people and situations, rather than cutting cords, something that never felt right to me.

The trouble with such courses is that many begin them, but never get past the first couple of lessons!

As this is something I am passionate about, I want people to have this method of feeling better available in their kit bag for life, because it is quick and very simple!

So, I have put the course into book form, so you have it all together to read and practice in one go!

In effect this is a workbook, with practice exercises. And this is something that is best practiced daily, as life throws things up. Practice otherwise can become dull and boring and make you less likely to turn to such tools as this, when needed.

Have fun delving into this method, and please, please use it! I KNOW it works!

Kirsten Ivatts

Acknowledgements

I wish to thank all of the people who have used my method of reclaiming energy to great effect in their lives, giving me the confidence that this was not just meant for me!

I would also like to thank my sister, Simone Ivatts, for all her help in proof reading my books and suggesting changes where needed.

Lastly I thank Silvia Hartmann, the inventor of modern energy techniques that incorporate, at their very core the two principles that are missing from so many other techniques…

LOVE and INTUITION.

The Download

For those who are not spiritually inclined, you may find most of this chapter doesn't agree with your world view. Please skip the paragraphs that make you feel uncomfortable. You don't need to be of on a spiritual path to reclaim your energy. However, you do need to be open minded enough to try something that makes little sense to the logical mind unless you have a keen understanding of the energetic systems of the human body.

I often get what I refer to as 'downloads' of information and energy in bed at night. I think of them as neural pathways opening to reveal new information from the vast databank that is available to all, if we were just aware enough to allow it. Some people call this the Akash and have rituals they use to access it.

I don't use a ritual. In 2012 while in meditation I was literally plugged in to this flow of data. My body lay down, physically and in the meditation, seemingly of its own accord. I often get some movement and adjustments to my posture when meditating, so this wasn't frightening. I had learned to go with the flow, so to speak!

Then a great river of light seemed to flow above me, and I was aware of tubes coming down from the river and plugging in to each chakra, including those outside of the physical body, and the palm and soles of the feet. It was an amazing feeling as the energy began coursing through me, and I lay for some time in ecstatic joy. Since that time, what before I called intuition, I now call data that I receive as ideas, words, understandings and guidance through being plugged into the light on all levels of my being.

I have found that many people access this pool of knowledge without knowing what they are doing. I don't think rituals are necessary, although to get the clearest information it helps to be open to receiving it and not blocking any 'downloads' by telling yourself you are just making it up.

People are far more magical than they believe! I teach and use many methods with other people, but the first thing they learn is TRUST. And it is a harder lesson than you may think, to fully trust in yourself.

In 2014 I got a significant download of information regarding energy. By this time, I was an Energy EFT Master Practitioner and was also using other energy methods alongside. I had learnt Chinese internal (or medical) Qi Gong with a very interesting Chinese man who treated my bed ridden mother for her rheumatoid arthritis. As a family we have known this man for many years, and he taught myself and my sister secret (Shaolin Temple) methods of meditation, breathing and Qi Gong, that build up energy in the Dan Tien, or store, as he called it. This is the region two fingers width below the belly button, and about two inches back into the body, where our life force energy resides. Through working with this man and learning Silvia Hartmann's intuitive methods of Energy Healing I had a good understanding of the energy systems and how important they are when it comes to any form of healing whatsoever. Once you understand how the energy body fits into the holistic equation, so many things make sense that never did before. Even now I get such a feeling of joy when

I work with a client and they suddenly have a huge AHA moment around why they are feeling how they do, and how easy it is to see a way to heal, when you bring energy into their awareness.

One part of this download that was very interesting related to cutting cords. Many people cut cords, to sever the connection on an energetic level to an event or person, but I have never liked it, it always felt wrong. Now I know why!

Before writing this, I tried to find out where this idea originated. I can't find it anywhere. What I am shown by my higher self is that, like many things we have adopted in Western culture from the Far East, some important information is missing. I have a sense that either something has been wrongly translated from texts, misunderstood by a student of some teacher or other, or that a huge bulk of information about this technique has simply been lost.

What I do know now is cutting cords is NOT the way to go about severing a connection with someone or something! Or rather, it is not a healthy way to do it. Neither can you release the energy that attaches you to others, or to events. The release happens, but from the other end. It happens when you draw the energy back into your own body. The release is a natural part of this process.

Let's use a past relationship as an example. Any relationship (or event) is not a one-way flow of energy, but a two-way dialogue, like a stream of data. It forms a connection between two people and the energy of both mingles together, creating a new set of data or energy that is the relationship. The relationship is something new, a recipe of parts.

When a relationship ends, some of the energy from each person remains locked into that relationship, and so is still mingling with that of the other person. You leave part of yourself behind. This can be felt in the negative feelings that occur on breaking up, feelings of loss, gaping holes in the stomach or chest (on an energy level these are real holes!), yearning for the other person. These are not just imagined; they are the physical feelings of missing energy. You are not missing the other person; however, you are missing energy that is YOURS!

In time these holes can be filled, but sometimes they remain, especially where grief is concerned. The longer these energetic wounds are open, the longer you suffer the emotional heartache, as well as creating new negative perceptions of the other person. But all of this is a symptom of energy that is missing, that you have left behind. Nothing more.

Now, cutting cords at this point causes a problem. You not only cut off the other person's energy, but you also cut off some of your own! And at the same time, you hang onto energy that doesn't belong to you! Do you see? Imagine the relationship energy is within a container. You walk away from that energy, and most of your energy goes with you (just how much depends on how much of yourself you put into the relationship). But the energy that is shaping that relationship container, the energy that you put in, remains. If you cut cords, you leave some of yourself behind. You may feel an initial lightening, but symptoms of energy loss will remain, and those wounds may heal on the surface, but the hole will still be there. This hole will create problems when you start a new relationship. And in general, grief will continue far longer than it needs to.

You know those bounce back relationships people have? That is a direct result of one of these holes that they are desperately trying to fill. And even if you wait a while before diving in again, most people will look for the energy they need to fill this hole, in another person. Not the best way to start any relationship…but a great way to further muddle up your energy system!

Any energy that you have drawn into yourself, through that relationship bubble remains there, even though it isn't yours. In the Magical Community of I, (another of my methods!) this energy would become a character with its own way of doing something, a way of speaking, a belief system, a judgement, a criticism, that isn't part of who you are. You have no business owning that, and it certainly won't help you in any way.

This happens a lot in childhood!

Any energy wants to go back to its source, so it will keep appearing to be released. If you ignore it, it will shout louder. Eventually, if you cannot recognize that it is not yours and find a way to release it, it will cause emotional, mental and physical issues. You lose track of who you are, why you are here, and end up a jumbled mess of energy. Think about how many relationships you have in a lifetime, platonic, romantic, familial. No wonder we all have issues!

Perhaps when humanity first learnt about cutting cords, they knew these things, and perhaps the information has been forgotten or simplified over time. But the way people swing their metaphorical swords to cut the ties that bind, does not work on the level it needs to.

Instead, what needs to be done is more akin to soul retrieval. We need to withdraw our energy from the relationship entity that was formed, and so, stop mingling with the energy of the other person, bringing it back to us, allowing for us to feel brighter, lighter, and fulfilled. This is empowering! This is just what you need when separating from someone. As your energy refills itself, there is no room for the energy that isn't yours and it is naturally released from your system.

You need your energy back! And so does the other person!

It might be wiser to not give away quite so much of ourselves in the first place, and once you understand this energy exchange, you will find that you gain awareness of how and when you do this, making it easier to put a stop to it before you feel the effects. And each time you reclaim your energy, you will realize how much better you feel and be more protective of it in future!

Let me be clear, this doesn't make you a less loving person. If anything, it increases the flow of love in your system. But instead of forcing your love onto another, which many of us are guilty of, you radiate love instead, which is better for you, and better for everyone around you.

I tried following the instructions I received to take back some energy from an area of conflict with my partner. Afterwards I felt bigger, stronger and I could see clearly where my boundaries lie, and I could state them without judgement, but instead with compassion for us both.

It was also shown to me, in this 'download' how this benefits the other person. When you withdraw your energy back into you, you stop the communication of data. It is like staying quiet in an argument. You are not breaking someone off in mid-sentence (something that creates more conflict), but instead you are keeping your words to yourself, which, in the case of an argument, gives the other person nothing to argue with. From an energy perspective, you are not clouding someone else's energy field with your own colours and perspectives, words and thoughts. Instead, you give them the gift of clarity and allow them to see life, and you, from an uncluttered perspective.

This is what letting go means, bringing your energy home from wherever you have left it, detaching at the other end by not being around anymore to continue the conversation, rather than cutting off the conversation in mid flow.

Isn't that an easier way to let go? How many times have you been told to let something, or someone go? Yet no one ever tells you how. There is just an assumption that you can cut yourself off from something and it will fall away. It doesn't work that way.

Let's look at a tree. When a tree lets go of its leaves each year it doesn't just decide to drop all the leaves and forget about them. It slowly withdraws its energy from them. It reclaims the energy back to where it is needed, in the very foundation of the tree, the center of energy that will keep the tree alive, healthy, and ready for a new surge of growth in the Spring. Nature will always show us the way to do something if we look closely enough.

So, next time someone says, 'Just let it go!', you know what to do. Go and reclaim your energy from the thing you want to let go of. Don't cut the leaf from the tree (cutting cords) and leave all that energy wondering what to do with itself now!

When you start thinking about all the places you have left energy, even if they were just ideas or thought processes, you can use this method in so many ways. And as you fill your energetic cup back up, and become stronger, life changes! And you become a very powerful and happy individual indeed.

Energy Systems

There is a lot of talk these days about energy vampires. An energy vampire is a person who seems to sap your energy. You will come away from such a person feeling literally drained. I have read so many different theories about protecting yourself from these types of people, and I have a few things to share of my own.

Firstly, I want to explain what energy protection really is all about. You can only be fully protected on an energetic level if your own energy is full, and flowing correctly, in, through and out. Putting a boundary in place around you isn't an effective solution. Boundaries keep things in as well as keeping things out. Imagine that an energy boundary is like a cell with no doors or windows. The air in there eventually will become stale and then oxygen will be depleted, and you will suffocate. Energetic boundaries work in the same way, except you would rarely manage to keep one in place for long enough for such an extreme to happen.

Energy can be likened to water. When water is flowing it stays clean, clear and fresh, and holds within it, life. It also keeps creating its own energy.

Still water soon goes stagnant. It becomes murky and clogged up with anything that falls into it. Your energy system, and the energy system of everything else is the same. When you have a brain fog, and you cannot see clearly, and feel down, you have stagnant energy. There is no flow. If you force yourself to go for a walk, you will begin to feel different. If you go for a walk outside, you will feel better. If you go for a walk somewhere very rural, woodland, or near a river or the sea you will feel better still.

Life force energy is far more readily available to us outdoors, away from the trappings of modern society. Rivers, oceans, fast flowing streams, forests, will all help your body to restore its depleted energy.

Like blood, energy can renew itself and produce more, but if your reserves are already low, or you've had stagnant energy for a long time the amount of energy input needed to revive you is massive. Think of a stagnant pond. How much water would it need to clear it? And how fast would it need to flow, to get rid of the debris?

Going back to energy protection, the only way to get rid of the negative energies of others, that have got into our system for whatever reason, is for our energy to be full, and fast flowing like a mountain river in spring. In this way the negatives are just washed away quickly and effectively.

If your energy is like the stagnant pond, and the majority of people are somewhere between this and the river analogy, the negativity of others will fall into the pond and sit on the bottom. That energy will taint your energy, making you feel confused, upset, unclear, unwell. And it will stay there and eventually your brain will decide it must be your energy, and you will take it on. From an energetic viewpoint this is one of the ways beliefs, habits, and perceptions come about.

If you are someone who would be classed as sensitive to energy, you will find that just being in the presence of other people can be unbearable. You are like an open door to their energy. You are the type of person who notices energy vampires and can become fearful of people because of this.

Crystals, visualizations, amulets and many other things may be suggested for you by well-meaning people who follow traditional methods. We have to remember that many traditional methods are lacking a lot of the original information. While these things can help a little, they are not a long term solution.

The only LONG TERM SOLUTION to energy vampires or negative energy is a fully functioning ENERGY SYSTEM.

Some people are described as thick skinned. The negativity of others doesn't seem to bother them, and they are usually very optimistic about life. Generally, these people will be energetic physically. Usually, people like this have a fast-flowing energy system. This doesn't mean that they will never become ill or down, but it does mean that they are far more likely to get over such things quickly.

After reading all of this you might be thinking there is no hope for you! Please don't! Retrieving energy you have left behind in people, places and events, and becoming energy aware, will help you rebuild your own unique energy, the energy that fits you exactly and makes you who you are.

Other things help too. Here is a short list. You can add to it when you find things that work for you.

• Drinking water (not out of plastic bottles)

• Getting outdoors to places that have high energy

• Exercise

• Doing the energy exercises on food to see what is best for you personally to eat.

• Meditation and deep tummy breathing

• Mindfulness practice/self-awareness

You know when your body is depleted, weak and beginning to show signs of illness. But most people are completely unaware of their energy system and how that looks and feels. Here is a tip. If your body is not feeling great or you have physical problems, your energetic body is five times worse. If we learn to detect our energy and put things right there, then the physical body has a much easier time of things!

Luckily it is easy to do things to start rebuilding the energy body, and eventually your efforts will show up in the physical body too. If you start with the physical body and ignore the energy body, repairs will be temporary, a band aid at best.

You will know you are helping your energy system, even though you can't see it, by how you feel. Your emotions will become balanced, you will feel happier, your head will be clearer, you will see solutions rather than problems, you will feel loved and want to give love. You will be less judgmental and more accepting of others and yourself.

If you are unsure of how to track your energy level changes, start now by writing in a journal how your energy would look now, if it was water. Is it stagnant and still, is there a trickle, a small stream or a rushing river?

As things change, keep thinking of the water analogy. If things are going well and you are a stream running calmly through a meadow, but then suddenly you feel like you have hit a pool and water isn't flowing so fast, then this is a sign that you just left some energy somewhere. Look at what has happened in your life and take that energy back **RIGHT NOW!**

The more you practice retrieving energy the quicker you will be able to do it. If someone is rude to me or judging and I feel that in my own system, I instantly attach a rainbow to the person and draw my energy right back, there and then. I usually blow them a golden kiss too. This can sometimes change the person in front of your eyes. Its magical when that happens!

Learning to never leave your energy behind, and to retrieve energy if you do is empowering. It is a simple and effective tool, and you are never without it! Unlike energy tapping, you can do it wherever you are without feeling conspicuous. Once you have done the initial exercises in this book, and have a better functioning energy system, you will find that energy returns to you instantly, and that you are aware of exactly when you give it away! This helps shift your focus from the negative energy sapping things to the positive energy giving things. And life becomes better, more exciting and fun!

Rainbows

There are lots of 'channels' you can use to reclaim your energy, but the one I personally use, and recommend is the rainbow method. This involves attaching a rainbow to the person or situation you are reclaiming energy from, and seeing it arc across into your own system.

But why the rainbow? Firstly, a rainbow is made up of light reflected off water droplets. Light equals energy, and water fits well with energy too. Secondly rainbows hold the 7 chakra colours that exist within the area of our physical body. This means that as you reclaim energy it can filter into the correct colour and from there, find its way into the place it is missing from.

Rainbows are also rather magical. They are something that lifts us, that we gaze on in wonder. I have never come across anyone so far, who holds any negative connotations to rainbows. And what is at the end of a rainbow? A pot of gold! That is exactly what you ae receiving as you gain all your energy back!

There is one more thing about rainbows. You can angle them so that the flow of energy is coming down hill, but in a manageable way. It is far easier to visualize the energy flow with this arc shape, slightly tilted to run down.

Relationships and the Method.

Human beings are masters of relationships. We don't just relate to other people; we create relationships with **EVERYTHING!**

Just think of your childhood, and the toys that became real to you. They became real because you began a relationship with them and gave that relationship some of your energy. Of course, this then made an inanimate object into a storied being, your focus gave it a place in the Universe, and it became alive for you. Some children will not sleep without their 'storied being' beside them. Parents should never tell a child that they are being ridiculous, and that the 'being' is just a teddy, or some such thing. In the child's reality the teddy is as real as anything else they are in a relationship with.

Over time the child grows, their energy changes, and they need different relationships. They naturally take their focus/energy away from a teddy, and place it elsewhere, perhaps in a cat or a dog or another child. This is a natural part of how we learn to relate to other things. Relationships with other conscious beings hold more focus as we grow, because they are more fascinating, and more challenging, and they make us think. It is harder to become bored, when you cannot control the responses of that which you are relating to.

We have the ability to put energy into everything, recreating these things as we go, into something new (think manifesting). It also means that when a collaboration of energies (relationship) goes sour, for whatever reason, our energy is affected, which means our emotions and thought processes and, ultimately, our actions and physical bodies are affected too.

We are relating, creating beings, and this continues from birth until death. The more aware we are of what is happening on an energy level, the more control we have, and the more we learn. As we learn we become more confident and eventually we become magical beings who know how to create their reality.

We are not separate from anything. On an energetic level we continually intermingle with other energy, to the point where we are just the energy of the Universe. It is our consciousness that shapes that energy into who we are on the material plane, coupled with the consciousness of those around us (how others see us), the conscious intent of our parents, especially around conception and birth, and the consciousness of the Universe (how the energy of the stars and planets were interacting with the energy on Earth at the time and place of your birth). And your own soul holds an intention of what it wants to achieve, or learn in this lifetime, through this unique human being. This is exciting and intriguing and has huge potential, but right now, we need to know how to pull back all those bits of us that we have left behind.

We need to regain control of our energy to feel good!

The best way to learn how to do this is to begin by practicing on relationships with other people, as they are the ones that we plough a lot of ourselves into, especially romantic relationships.

We all know the feelings that are created when we meet someone and go through the process of falling in love. The energies of each person, literally dance together, weaving in and out, creating an entity that becomes the relationship. The feelings that flow back into our physical body are amazing! We never want these feelings to end. These feelings are caused by very fast moving positive energy. It creates a sensation of ecstasy and joy, and love. However, you cannot keep using your energy up in this way, otherwise you become physically depleted, and so the intensity of the dance slows, and the feelings become less intense, allowing the physical body to sleep, eat, and rest.

When I first met my twin flame partner, we exhausted ourselves with this dance. There was so much joy at our re meeting, and re-membering that after the first two weeks (where there was virtually no physical contact), our physical bodies needed rest. When eventually we were together all the time, we spent as much time sleeping as we did anything else! Be warned!!

When we are part of the dance we are working at a higher vibration, and all we can see is the goodness in the other person. We are highly attracted to them, and both sides have high focus on the other, investing energy into the relationship entity. At this point we can feel that we are not separate from the other person, indeed the whole world seems a magical place to be in, and we can see (if we are aware of such things) our connection to everything. This is natural when you vibrate at a higher frequency of light.

The human body is not designed to do this for long periods of time. It can be trained to up this frequency, and if you think of the abilities that some highly trained Qigong Masters have, or Buddhists Monks, you can see how long it can take to do this. The average human body cannot take such high levels of joy over an extended period without breaking down, just as it can't take any high levels of sadness, anger or fear. There must be balance within the energy system.

Once the relationship gets past the initial high frequency period, and the energy in your own system slows, you begin to see where you are separate from the other person. This shows you what you don't like about them, what irritates you, you see their humanness and not their soul. We often yearn to feel that initial closeness again and that makes it hard for us to be apart from them. We are not actually wanting to be with them, we are wanting to experience our connection to everything, which we found through our energy dance with them.

The human brain just tells us it is them we need, because this is how it is programmed. If you begin to understand how energy works, you can learn to be separate from those you love, and still feel whole. In energy terms there is no time, no space, no boundaries between us and anything else. It is the ego that makes us think we are separate. The ego is like a program that runs to allow our soul to experience separateness, so that it can learn and grow. You can bypass the program if you advance enough!

Of course, all of this is happening to the other person in the relationship too, and both sides allow the ego to begin the game of judgement, and the energy that is now filtering into the relationship is changing its tone. It isn't all about love anymore; it's more about what your ego thinks you want from that other person and how you want that person to be. Some of that energy is so thick and heavy, it creates walls of defense and you become far less visible to each other than you were. Literally, you cannot feel that soul energy that you felt at the beginning.

A relationship doesn't need to end, to start hurting you. The wall of defense can be felt by both parties and can make you both feel cut off from the other, as if there is suddenly distance between you. Of course, this is true from an energy viewpoint! There is literally a wall of energy, that is heavy, and dense.

There are as many reasons why a relationship suffers conflicts and challenges as there are relationships! The thing is, the reasons don't matter. What matters is to recognize that you can do something about it. And if the relationship ends, the best way to avoid hurt and conflict is to retrieve your energy straight away! Then both sides will feel better.

So, let's try this.

I want you to think back to a recent conflict with someone, preferably a romantic partner. If you haven't had a recent one, go back to one that springs to mind, or choose someone close to you that is a friend or family member.

Take a minute to revisit the event in your mind. As you do this, remember certain phrases or words used in the conflict and try and connect with how this event made you feel IN YOUR BODY.

As an example, a recent argument with my partner hit me bang under my rib cage. The feeling was so intense that it was a physical pain. But as we are all individuals, we feel the emotional energy or the stress of a conflict in our own way. So really take time to look at where you MOST felt the impact. As you get used to doing this, you will be aware of this happening in arguments and know that you must take back your energy straight away!

This place of impact is where the energetic connection between you and that other person exists, at that particular time. It is where the energy left your body, and now needs to return. Another conflict or person could affect a different area of your body. What is interesting is often certain WORDS get you in the same place every time, no matter who says them. This is a sign that an EVENT in the past, where these words were first hurled at you as negative energy, needs clearing. We will discuss events in another chapter.

The next step is to bring up an image of the conflict itself. Again, take a few moments to conjure it up in the mind's eye. Where were you, what was around you, were there other people nearby? Make sure the other person is also in the image. (If this is too painful, please try this on a different relationship. If you wish to work through it with my support, please contact me).

Got it?

Now we need to create a pathway, or a bridge, between the place of impact and the person within the event itself. We use a bit of visualization here and find out what works best for you.

Close your eyes and place a hand, or a finger, on your body where you can feel the energy is missing and needs to return. Then imagine a rainbow going from the image of the other person in the scene, TO this place in your body.

If the rainbow is not something that feels good, or makes sense to you, here are a number of other suggestions that work for people.

• A tunnel or channel that you see as open ended

• A funnel

• A bridge made of anything you want

• A rope

• A beam of light

You can experiment with any of these or see if your mind brings up a different suggestion.

Once you have connected your chosen pathway for the energy, ask out loud to reclaim all the energy you left behind in this event and with that person, via the link you have made.

Speaking out loud is important. It helps connect the logical mind with the creative mind and the subconscious (the mind that exists outside of our normal awareness levels, and runs all our programs that keep us alive, our beliefs, learnt behaviours etc). It helps the mind differentiate between your energy, the energy of the event itself and that of the other person. You only want your own energy back!

Now sit back and start to visualize the energy flowing back to you. You can just know it is on its way, or you can SEE it, of feel it. My energy is golden and sparkly! See what yours looks like. Be interested in this energy, take notice of it, be excited by it. After all, it is a part of you!

The most important thing at this stage is that you start to FEEL it entering back into your body at the place where it left. Focus on this area and any feelings or sensations that are occurring. Note what it does, where it flows to next and how you begin to feel. Most importantly...

Keep the energy flowing.

Sometimes you may feel pain, discomfort or some other negative feeling as the energy begins to come back. This is normal and shouldn't last more than a minute or two. Keep the flow going and make sure you don't block it at this point. It is easy to tense up and create a wall. Try moving around or wiggling that part of your body to make the energy move more quickly and to keep the muscles from contracting. You can also massage the spot. And be patient with yourself. If it doesn't happen straight away, relax, imagine, and enjoy until it does!

You will know when this process is finished. Firstly, you won't be able to feel the spot of discomfort anymore, and sometimes the bridge or vehicle for the energy disappears and you cannot imagine it back. Secondly, you will feel full of the most amazing energy. It is hard to describe how wonderful this feels. It is empowering, like being on top of the world. You may want to dance, hug someone, sing, but most importantly, you will not feel any negative emotion around the person or event anymore.

A really nice gesture, and one that I feel seals the deal, as it were, is to let a small amount of this new energy you now feel drift back to the person, before sealing shut your energy field. I like to imagine some of this energy on the palm of my hand, and then I blow it, like a kiss, to the person. Think of it as gratitude for what you shared, good or bad, and the lessons you learnt from your relationship. It is an offering of forgiveness, thanks and love and an acknowledgement that we all do our best, or what we think is our best at the time.

Lastly imagine shutting a door over the place the energy entered or sealing it off in some way that feels right for you.

When you regain energy, you will have a cognitive shift, and be able to see the conflict from a higher perspective and understand why each of you said and did what you did. This new understanding promotes feelings of forgiveness, but the conflict itself will hold no emotional charge for you. In fact, it may just drift from your mind altogether.

If these things do not happen, or don't happen to this degree, there is still energy left in the situation or with the person. That's OK. You can go back and redo this again!

Some conflicts are huge or have become huge because of the amount of time the energy has been missing. It may take a few goes at this to get all your energy back. There are also times when you begin to realize that the energy needs to come back from other conflicts as well, that are connected to this one in some way. As you gain more energy, energy flows more quickly and is stronger in your system. This gives you greater clarity about yourself, your issues, and other people.

There are times when you feel more than one place in your body when doing this. Focus on connecting to the place in which you feel the MOST discomfort. If, once you have done this in one spot, you can still feel the event somewhere else, then, repeat the technique linking that area as well. It may be that certain things that were said impacted you differently for many reasons.

It is a good idea to keep a journal when learning this technique. Write down:

• What your link looked like to the other person

• Where you felt the energy in your body

• How the energy felt as it came back to you

• What you felt like afterwards

• What new knowledge you gained from it

Once you have learnt the method to retrieve lost energy, apply it straight away after any negative issue arises in any relationship. This will stop any ongoing damage to you, your relationships, and other people.

Events

Events have an energy of their own. This energy is a combination of all the people who were there and how they were feeling, including you. It also contains energy from similar past events that you bring to THIS event as a means of reference for your own understanding. And the same goes for any other people that are there! It can also include the energy of the place where the event happened.

In other words, lots of energy can be intermingled in one event. But, of course, we only want to retrieve what is ours, which uncomplicates things somewhat, and we do that in the exact same way as we did it for a relationship.

Let's begin by thinking of an event, and it's easiest if you do this exercise with an event that happened recently. It doesn't need to be anything that you would label trauma; it could just be something that happened that caused you concern (or may still be doing so). As you get better at this, you can retrieve your energy from bigger events and those that have plagued you for years. But let's start simple!

I will give an example from my own life. This is a very small, everyday event that happened recently, that you might not even consider an event – in fact, you might not even consider it at all. But it impacted my energy body and my emotions (and I am very aware of my own energy), and a build-up of these impacts can change our perception and become a big energy blockage. By catching these small events, we can stop this happening. And small, recent events are very quick and easy to retrieve the energy from.

I will use this event to show you how I retrieve the energy.

A couple of weeks ago, my partner was away, and I felt unwell. Our relationship is a very close bond of energy, very intermingled, going back through many lifetimes. We vibrate at the same frequency, even though we are very different in how we deal with life. He was busy, working long hours and he didn't call as often as I thought he should, and he didn't message and ask how I was. Sounds ridiculous to be bothered by this, right? It is, but at that time, that event made me feel even more unwell, and I can still feel its impact now, so it NEEDS clearing! (Notice how this is an event that you would write off in your mind? But if you can still feel it, you are missing some energy. You left it behind!).

Often when we are unwell physically it impacts our emotional, mental and energetic wellbeing. My energy system was working harder than normal trying to clear negative energy from my system. When we are in a close bonded relationship, with someone who is on the same frequency, we borrow their energy when we need it, and vice versa. Because he was busy, and his focus was all on work, I could feel the energy that would normally be supporting me was missing. To my brain, and ego that became an emotional need. When you don't understand this, it is easy to start blaming that other person for how you feel. The brain then leaps in to add to this, perhaps with jealousy, anger, sadness, or anything else that would help to create the situation and make it into something it's not. And if you allow this to happen, suddenly it's real! You feel hurt, have a go at the other person, decide what is really happening, and WHOA…you have a conflict on your hands! How many times has this happened to you?

Let's repeat the process that we used before, using my own experience.

I can feel this event in my back, in my spine, just below the shoulder blades. It reaches deep inside to the middle of my chest.

Because I am remembering an event, I need to make this event into something to which I can attach my rainbow connection. My partner wasn't even there remember, I was on my own, so attaching it to him won't work. There are a couple of ways to do this.

4. You can make a shape with your hands, as if you were holding a ball. Into that ball, you can put all your memories of the event, especially emotions, and then seal it shut. This ball is then the entity of the event that you can connect to.

2. You can visualize the event in your head as a ball, or whatever shape it wishes to be, as long as it is contained. Simply ask the mind, out loud, what shape is this event? Mine is triangular. This entity may have different colours,

movement within, or it may not stay one shape, but keep morphing. As long as you can connect your link to it, it really doesn't matter.

Now that I have my triangular entity with everything I felt and could remember from the event within, I can easily see the rainbow coming from it and attaching to me at the point in my back. Although it takes time to describe, it takes seconds to do all of this!

Out loud I now say,

'I wish to reclaim all of my energy from this event with my partner not ringing enough or asking how I felt.'

There is a pain in my back as I do this, and a feeling like a bubble that needs to rise in my chest, an opening that needs to come out. My thoughts are on how I had felt uncared for, but then I realize that this event is not the first, there have been others, very similar, and I am actually drawing my energy back from all of these events.

I say out loud,

'I wish to take back all of my lost energy from every time I felt uncared for when any partner didn't phone, text or seem to care enough when away.'

I wiggle my back to help keep this connection open. There is pressure in my chest and back now, and then suddenly, it is like this 'hole' that was causing pressure becomes a beautiful and uplifting feeling in my upper body. There is still a slight pain where it enters on my back, so I keep the connection. At the same time, a fog lifts from my mind, and I feel compassion for him struggling to juggle my needs with those of work, and the stresses of being away.

Bringing this energy in has made me realize that it is pushing out energy that was stuck and needs release. I let the rainbow flow into my body and open up a channel, up into my throat and back of my neck, into the bones at the base of my skull, and now the pain can rise up this channel (I could FEEL that the energy needed to go that way – I didn't use my mind to decide ,but let the energy itself show me). I can feel it in the back of my head, pressure, tension, rising up and out behind my ears. Gone.

I now seal the place on my back, with a big golden plug!

Wow, something that I expected to take a minute at the most, took five! There were many little events that had made this most recent one a physical reality, in that I could still feel it. See what I mean about ignoring all those little events that we brush off so quickly, but can in fact add up to something bigger?

Now that I am finished, the memories of this event are sliding away, becoming nothing. I have removed my energy from it and so it no longer exists.

And hey presto! The phone rings, and it is my partner (who was away last night)! This is something that I find quite magical about doing this. When your energy leaves an event, anyone, even unwittingly, caught up in that event, even if they were not aware of it or physically present, feels the relief too, feels more open to you, and responds positively. Magical!

I want you to try this, with something small and recent, that may seem silly, but something that still sticks in your mind and can still be felt physically.

As you get better at this, you can begin to do the same procedure with bigger events, from further back, with more trauma attached. Some big events are very difficult to do alone, and you may need help with these. Please call on an experienced Energist for help in such cases.

This exercise is also good at making us aware of how many times we create an event out of nothing, and this new event impacts us emotionally and physically. The more times you can take your energy back from an event as soon as it happens, the clearer and brighter your energy system will be, and you will see how easy it is to manifest your reality!

Guiding Stars

Energists are aware that it is not only bad events that cause us problems. Silvia Hartmann coined the term GUIDING STARS in her amazing work on modern energy techniques, to cover seemingly good events that never evolved as far as they should, and so, in their own way, left a problem within the energy system, because the energy became stuck.

An example of a guiding star event would be someone who had a wonderful time the first time they tried a cigarette. This caused an energy spike in their energy body, and a euphoric feeling, and from then on, each cigarette is really an attempt to recapture that moment. This is similar to what I discussed in the relationships chapter about the initial, amazing feelings a new relationship brings on. This puts a whole new spin on issues such as addiction and if you ever decide to learn something like Modern Energy Tapping, Events Psychology or EMO (Energy in Motion), created by Silvia Hartmann for the Guild of Energists, you will learn more about Guiding Stars.

If we leave energy behind in an event, then it doesn't make any difference whether that event impacted us in a positive or negative way. It's just energy, and it's just an event.

So, let's try and recapture that wonderful energy that we left behind in a good event, then we don't have to keep looking for it everywhere else!

36

I want you to think of something that you can remember the feeling of. Perhaps it was a wedding, a special Christmas or birthday, or something else that left you feeling wonderful.

Take some time to recapture that event in your mind. Try and remember how you felt, even if you can only describe it, rather than really feeling it yet in your body.

Now close your eyes, breathe deeply and relax.

Because we are remembering an event, we need to make this event into something that we can attach a connection to. Here is a recap of what to do.

1. You can make a shape with your hands, as if you were holding a ball. Into that ball, you can put all your memories of the event, especially emotions, and then seal it shut, visualizing a ball to connect to.

2. You can visualize the event in your head as a ball, or whatever shape it wishes to be, as long as it is contained. Simply ask the energy mind, out loud, what shape this event is.

Now ask yourself where in your body the energy from this event needs to return to, and then attach your energy channel from the event to that point in your body.

Say out loud,

'I wish to retrieve all of my energy that I left behind in this wonderful event!'

Then simply allow the energy to start coming back, feeling it as it flows into different areas in the body. If you like, you can run through the event from start to finish in your mind, like replaying a movie, and see if this helps the energy to keep flowing.

Remember to wiggle and move about as the energy returns, so that the flow has somewhere to go, and doesn't get stuck.

Once you feel there is nothing more to retrieve, seal up the place in your body where the energy entered, and sit for a while and see how you feel.

Try doing this especially at times where you are feeling low or depressed.

You can also try this exercise with anything you suspect you use as a support mechanism, like food, alcohol, cigarettes, marijuana. Try and remember your first event with this thing when you felt euphoria. It is that event that you need to connect to, no matter how far back it was. Food that is used as a comfort mechanism is often linked to a childhood event where you felt nurtured, loved or supported. It is that lovely guiding star event that holds your energy still, but your brain associates it with food, so when you feel low, or unloved, you eat!

I found that I linked red wine (not the cheap stuff…good red wine), to a time when I was pretty low, and I went to stay at my father's house (security). He always had very good red wine from a wine merchant. While I was there, he had a dinner party. I had a great time, socialized, felt loved, at peace, and fulfilled…and drank a lot of wine.

For years after I drank GOOD red wine when I felt I needed nurturing or security, which logically makes no sense (often costing me money I didn't have!), but my brain had linked the two things together! The energy of the event became stuck in my system, as an energetic imprint, or memory, that I wanted to replicate. If I had gone to my fathers at that time feeling fine, with a healthy flowing energy system, the energy of that evening would have kept flowing, and never become stuck. Energy becomes stuck when our energy is going slowly and is thick and heavy. When it is light, and we are full of energy, it completes the cycle of in, through and out, and we don't hold onto any emotional issues, good or bad. We enjoy them and let them go.

Remember to record what happens in your journal when doing these exercises. Ask yourself questions like:

1. How did this feel? Was it any different to the other exercises?

2. How did you feel once this was completed?

3. When remembering the event, has anything changed?

4. Was this easier, harder, or about the same as reclaiming energy from a negative seeming event?

Concepts

There are certain concepts in life that we all throw a lot of energy into. The two biggest ones are LOVE and MONEY. Yet these two things are just energy.

By leaving energy behind in these, and any other concept, we stay continually focused on them. Our minds can't leave them alone. We feel a constant need for both to feel whole and secure. Our energy, which is a mixture of countless events, plus our own unique energy we were born with, plus the energy we hold onto that isn't even our own, masks the original concept. For example, if you have had bad experiences with money, or grew up in a household where money was lacking, your energy within the concept of money is going to be negative. Your relationship with money will be clouded by your own beliefs. If you remove your energy from the concept of money, you will start to see money differently, noticing things about it that you didn't see before.

So, let's have a go at removing all the energy we have left behind in LOVE and in MONEY. Once you have tried these two big obvious ones, try other things like appearance, happiness, life purpose, or even… GOD!

We each have our own perception of all of these concepts, based on things that have happened over time, and what we were told, or learned, of these things as children, and we add to this perception with our energy until these concepts can rule our lives!

When you sit down to do these exercises, leave yourself a good amount of time. These could be life changing for you, and you don't want to miss out on the experience. Also, most concepts are created by many different events over your lifetime, so a lot of energy needs to return!

Here is the best way I have found to do this.

First, sit somewhere comfortable, quiet, and where you won't be disturbed. Take a few moments to relax, breathe, and get comfy.

Now I want you to ask out loud,

'Show me the concept I hold of....'

Let an image appear in your mind. Be aware of where it is in relation to you. Is it in touching distance or further away? Is it above your head, to one side, right in front of you? If you can stabilize the image by knowing exactly where it is, it helps to bring back the energy.

Now take a good few moments, really looking at the image of the concept. Talk about how it looks out loud. As an example, the concept of LOVE to me is right in front of me, merged into my body. It reaches up about a foot past the top of my head, and down to my knees. It is magenta coloured with soft rose pink swirls. And it feels supportive, warm, inviting, nourishing.

Can you see how describing the image you have of the concept can help bring it into being? It is far easier to take back energy from something that you can see and feel to this extent.

Next, say,

'I now wish to reclaim all the energy I have left behind in the concept of......'

Ask yourself where in your body the energy needs to return to, and then see your energy channel or rainbow coming from the concept to that point in your body. You may need to do this a few times for a few different parts of the body. Keep the channel open and feel how the energy flows. All the while be aware of the concept and see how it changes.

Only do one concept in a day. Try and give yourself a bit of time in between to see how your awareness, thoughts and feelings around the concept changes. And make sure to write it all down! It might take a few days for this type of work to really filter into your understanding and create that cognitive shift.

And finally, approach this as a bit of fun. Don't go into this feeling like you are on some sort of mission. Play with it, expect to get something good from it, and if you don't, don't worry. Leave it a few days and try again. Sometimes we shield ourselves so heavily from things like LOVE and MONEY that it takes a few attempts to break through. Be gentle with yourself and ask for help if you need it.

Good luck!

Here is something that I found out when doing this exercise on money. I share it so that you can see how your perception of something can change.

I began by seeing a globe, as my money entity. It was very heavy and solid and lots of people seemed to be in it. As I took my energy back from this concept my vision of it gradually changed. The globe became huge, and light, golden and full of swirling energy. There were hardly any people here. I could still see the other globe, but it was further away from me, and I wasn't connected to it anymore.

I felt drawn to step into this vision to find out more. I entered into the globe, and it was full of what I can only describe as a light and abundant energy that I floated on, completely supported by it.

The understanding that came to me was deep and hard to put into words. The first, heavy globe was how most people perceive money. It was like the hive mind perspective of it, heavy, hard work, not easy to connect with. The second globe was the real energy behind money. It was light, abundant, readily available and supportive. I felt that it was largely devoid of people because the majority of humanity isn't tuning into that energy at all, but rather the first heavier globe. It made me realize that I thought of money as a necessary evil, hard work, heavy, hard to connect with, and

I can tell you now, the second globe was a far nicer experience. Now when I connect to the concept of money, I connect to the second globe!

You might be wondering why the image changed. As you take back more of your energy, you actually become lighter, not heavier. You become less dense, clearer, and this brings clarity of perception. As I became lighter, my perception of money changed, and I could then tune into an energy that I had never had before. This also proved to me that using this method of energy retrieval helps us to grow as Souls in a human body, without spending years in meditation. We are being gifted an acceleration of our understanding and evolution on this planet. This isn't the only method coming through, many people are getting downloads of information these days. Your role is to find the method that fits you best, and perhaps, as you are reading this book, you are being given a sign that this method is for you.

Places and Other Things

At the beginning of this book, I mentioned how we create relationships with everything, and that includes places and things. As any relationship requires an energy input, we are more than likely to walk away from these relationships leaving a part of us behind.

It took me a long time to get over a house I had lived in, and the garden surrounding it that I had created, and the hills surrounding that. I had ploughed a lot of time and energy into that place, and until I retrieved that energy a few years later, no house felt like a home.

The same can be true of things. We often say we have become attached to something. That attachment is the energy we have put into it. When the item is no longer around, we need that energy back! Wedding and engagement rings can still hold attachment even when the relationship is over, items of jewelry that you lose, books, ornaments, cuddly toys, handbags, clothes, cars... you can go on and on and on! People become attached to almost anything. Sometimes this attachment becomes an obsession, or an addiction, and even a fetish! Yet all we need to do to move on is remove our energy from the item.

Try thinking of a place that you have strong memories of, good or bad. Conjure up an image of the place and try to feel it too. Really put all your senses into taking you there. There will probably be one area in the place that you remember very clearly. Attach your energy connection to that area and then follow it all the way back to wherever this place impacts your body.

As before, say out loud,

'I wish to reclaim all the energy I have left behind in this place.'

Then let the energy flow!

You can do exactly the same with an object. If you no longer have the object, imagine it. If you DO have it, then sit it in front of you. Follow the same procedure to bring back your energy. Keep a record in your journal that covers what changes for you, about the place or the object. Try this with places and objects you like and ones you don't. If you have focused on them at some point, then you have probably left energy behind with them.

Food.

You can try this also with food that you wish you didn't like to eat so much of, or food that you have decided you don't like, even though it is supposed to be good for you! Food is only good or bad because of your perception of it. Really food is just energy, and energy just is. There is no good or bad energy, there is only your perception of energy and what you have created with it.

As I mentioned before, food can be linked to an event, but it can also be linked to something you read, overheard or were told. We are all told that cakes and chocolate taste wonderful, but are bad for us, so we are pre-programmed with this information. What if we were told the same thing about cabbage, or sprouts? How would we perceive these foods then? What if we grew up being told chocolate was awful, but you should eat it as it would help stop cancer and other illnesses?

When you understand that we are just energy, and food is just energy, and there is no good or bad energy, then really that last paragraph makes no sense.

Because our energy system is unique to each of us, then it makes sense that the energy of different foods is unique to each of us. The best way to find out what food works for you and what doesn't, is to take your energy away from food and see what happens. If you have food issues, begin by taking energy back from the concept of food and see if your vision and feelings about food changes. Like mine did with money.

Then take your energy back from foods that you think cause you a problem. You may find that these are different foods to the ones you would have chosen before you took energy back from the concept of food!

You can do the same with drinks, vitamins, medicines, holistic therapies, exercise, literally anything that affects you physically that you will have preconceived ideas about, that were never actually your own ideas at all. Try taking your energy back from your scales too!

Animals

So many of us have relationships with animals that it seems silly not to give them a section. Family pets are companions, and sometimes surrogate babies, and we pour a lot of energy into our animal relationships. When it comes time to part with these animals, for whatever reason, we can really suffer the loss. By retrieving the energy from the animal, you can, of course, feel better very quickly.

This doesn't mean that you will forget a pet that has died or had to be rehomed; it just means that you can cope with it because you have a full quota of energy! The more I write this book, the more I realize what energy litter louts we really are!

But there is something else that we do unknowingly when we create a relationship, and this especially affects animals and children. Perhaps because they are less likely to put up defenses in the way adults do. We transmit our concerns and our stresses to them, especially if those concerns involve the animal or child in some way.

Animals have much better-defined ESP than humans and use energy exchanges to communicate. Because all animals still have some natural instinct that goes back to a time before their domestication, they have very direct and powerful ways to communicate danger to each other.

As humans, we imagine danger at every given opportunity, and the link we have to our animals passes this alert on. This can cause both ourselves and the animal, problems.

Animals fear that which causes them danger, like another bigger animal, or an aggressive animal, (or a leaf on the breeze if the animal is a thoroughbred horse!) These are all reasonable dangers. Animals don't start off fearing anything unless they have an experience that they perceive might bring them physical harm.

Yet I have known animals that show stress symptoms for no reason. Nine times out of ten these animals are actually presenting me with the stress that their owner is feeling. For a while I used Emotional Freedom Technique on animals. In most cases I ended up using it on the owner, and the animals righted themselves.

Changes in behaviour, training problems, changes in eating habits, can all be a side effect of your energy affecting the animal. By removing your energy from the animal regularly, you can help combat the stress on both of you!

Your lack of energy is more likely to cause you added worry, even if you don't feel you have less physical energy. And, of course, all of that stress energy is going to become a problem in a highly receptive receiver, such as an animal. Dogs and horses both live in social groups, and their senses are designed to be aware of the pack and the herd. This is how they survive. If your energy is constantly stressed, your dog will be constantly on the lookout for danger, which can cause many behavioural issues. If you fret your dog isn't eating as much as the packet says it should, the dog will wonder why you are stressed about the food, and either think you want it for yourself, or think there is something wrong with it!

Be energy aware when it comes to your animals and retrieve your energy from them regularly!

While we are talking about animals, I just want to add a little about the focus of energy from many people on, let's say, an animal that is on the endangered species list. While we need to be aware of where we, as humans, are playing a part in the problems different species have, we also need to be aware of the negative effects so much focused energy can have.

Energy is powerful. We know that prayer can have an amazing effect when used with enough intention and by enough people. But this same attention, focusing on the PROBLEMS facing a species, can also be powerful in a negative way. If you really want to help an animal species, don't read or listen to all the negative talk. There is no way that you can read that and feel good. And so, there is no way you can create a better world for that animal! If everyone is focusing their worry on elephants, elephants are going to suffer. It is better to take your energy away from the concept of all the things elephants suffer from, as this will bring clarity and you might actually find a solution to their problems!

Remove your energy from the animal, or rather the concept or entity that the media has created around that animal, and then just send it pure love. If you want to help a charity, that is fine, but send your money from this place of love, and not with the feelings of dread or anxiety about the animal.

This goes for people in need too. By focusing all our negative feelings (those created by feeling sorry for their plight), on these people, we do not help! In fact, we make things worse. We add to the negative energy surrounding them! Take your energy back! And then send them love.

Children

One of the most beneficial things you can give to your child is an awareness of energy and how a positive and negative perspective of energy affects them and the world around them. By doing this, you empower them! By teaching them how to take their energy out of a relationship, or event, entity or concept, place or thing, you give them a massive boost and start the next generation off with a full quota of energy to play with.

What does that do?

It creates people who know how to deal with life's stresses, and so spend more time feeling happy and clear-headed than angry, frustrated or fearful, with no idea what to do when something goes wrong.

In my opinion, schools should teach this first and foremost. If we can begin by giving our children such a fantastic start in life, then there is hope for the future education system, and from there, the world!

It may sound like a huge leap, but it really is possible, and children understand energy where adults struggle. It is very easy to teach children energy techniques such as this, and they very easily feel the positive effects.

When it comes to your relationship with children, remember that like animals, children are very energy aware and tuned in to the feelings of others. This is why an already stressed mother will spend the day dealing with a crying baby, or a stressed-out teacher will hand out more detentions than a relaxed and happy one. Children respond more to how you FEEL than what you say or do. If you are having issues with a child, stop looking for the answers in them, and start looking for the answers in you. Retrieve your energy from the relationship you have with them, and then send them love in its place. Do this regularly and notice the difference in the child and how you deal with them.

We are so quick to look outside of ourselves when it comes to problems, and not recognize the energy we are giving out or putting into our relationships. And the more we put out and leave behind in all these many places, the more lost, confused and stressed we become!

Retrieve all that lost energy and start feeling like YOU again!

Creating Positives

We have talked in this book about retrieving our energy, left behind in an energetic relationship. More often than not, we feel the need to retrieve energy from negative situations, so I began thinking, why not just create positive situations instead!

It's easier said than done, but as usual, practice and awareness go a long way into making this a reality.

Here is a simple example that everyone can relate to. You have a dentist visit booked and you know there is work to be done. Every time that you think about this visit, some form of negative feeling arises. What you are doing here is feeding a future event with negative energy!

Instead, as soon as you book the appointment, retrieve your energy from it. There WILL be some to retrieve and it probably has origins in past events at the dentist! Then open up a new channel between you and the event. Imagine how you would like the appointment to go, how you want to feel before, during and after! Let all of that beautiful positive energy flow from you to the event. Keep allowing this flow until you begin to feel great inside! Until you are excited about the event, until you look forward to going!

Over the coming days, if you start to feel bad again, or any little anxieties emerge, deal with them straight away, using the method above.

It only takes one experience of how much this can change a future event to make you realize just how powerful you are and just how much you can affect your life and what happens in it!

Next, try this on a relationship, a job interview, a new house, an exam, anything! You really can make a difference, and the more you practice, and the more times you experience the difference YOU created, the more control you will gain over what happens in your life. It is like the small stone rolling down the hill that creates the avalanche. But this avalanche is a cascading cornucopia of fantastic positive energy that you will never want to stop creating!

Please try this today!

And of course, you might reach a point where you have no energy left to retrieve, when you never leave energy littered everywhere you have been, and you only ever send positive energy forward!

What a life that will be!

OTHER BOOKS

HOW TO READ
ORACLE CARDS
For Self Help and Enlightenment

by Kirsten Ivatts

Available as a paperback or Kindle on Amazon, and as an eBook on most other devices including Apple.

Praise for How To Read Oracle Cards

Absolutely love this little book, Kirsten goes into the oracle so deeply and this will now always be my go to oracle guidance. Thank you Kirsten...look forward to more of your books. Highly recommend.

This book really helped me to trust my intuition when working with Oracle cards.

This book is an easy to use, yet deep guide to using Oracle cards as a self-help tool in everyday life. Kirsten shares her learning from 25 years of working with Oracle cards, but where this book differs from, and improves upon, others I have read on this subject is in teaching us how to fully connect with our intuitive self to enhance our understanding of the cards, something which has grown out of her work as an Energist. Kirsten illustrates her teachings with examples from her own experiences and sets practical exercises for the reader in each section. She also shares different types of card spreads to try, both when doing readings for yourself and for others, as well as hints, tips and useful links. An inspiring and exciting book that provides practical and easily followed guidance on how to better understand ourselves and others using the popular and accessible divination tool of Oracle cards.

Good little book. Useful information in getting how to know and understand the cards before working with them. On getting a new deck one wants to work with the cards straightaway, this book gets you to understand your own connection to the cards. Really found it interesting!

Yet another amazing self help journey Kirsten takes us on with this 'How to Read Oracle Cards' book. Her techniques are so unique you'll find yourself exploring inner depths and realms you only previously imagined. This book is a door to a new journey you're gonna want to take.

CONTACT INFORMATION

EMAIL: Kirsten@kirstenivatts.com

WEB: https://kirstenivatts.com

FACEBOOK

Printed in Great Britain
by Amazon